13 Colonies

MASSACHUSETTS

13 Colonies

MASSACHUSETTS

THE HISTORY OF MASSACHUSETTS COLONY, 1620–1776

ROBERTA WIENER AND JAMES R. ARNOLD

Raintree

Chicago, Illinois

For information, address the publisher:
Raintree, 100 N. LaSalle, Suite 1200, Chicago, IL 60602

Printed in China by South China Printing.
09 08 07 06
10 9 8 7 6 5 4 3 2

Library of Congress Cataloging-in-Publication Data
Wiener, Roberta, 1952-
 Massachusetts / Roberta Wiener and James R. Arnold.
   p. cm. -- (13 colonies)
Includes bibliographical references (p.) and index.
Contents: Plymouth Colony -- Massachusetts in 1620 -- Massachusetts Bay Colony -- Colonial life in Massachusetts --
A growing population leads to war -- The English government exerts control -- The French and Indian War -- A matter of taxes --
From boycott to battlefield -- Glossary.
  ISBN 0-7398-6881-0 (lib. bdg.) -- ISBN 1-4109-0305-2 (pbk.)
  ISBN 978-0-7398-6881-2 (lib. bdg.) -- ISBN 978-1-4109-0305-1 (pbk.)
 1. Massachusetts--History--Colonial period, ca. 1600-1775--Juvenile literature. 2. Massachusetts--History--1775-1865--Juvenile literature. [1. Massachusetts--History--Colonial period, ca. 1600-1775. 2. Massachusetts--History--1775-1865.] I. Arnold, James R. II. Title. III. Series: Wiener, Roberta, 1952- 13 colonies.
 F67.W66 2004
 974.4'02--dc22
                    2003021144

Disclaimer

Some words are shown in bold, **like this.** You can find out what they mean by looking in the glossary.

Title page: A view of Boston in 1657. Massachusetts grew rapidly. In 1695 there were 83 towns on the colony's tax list. By 1765, there were 186, of which Boston was by far the largest.

Opposite: The abundant fishing off the coast of Massachusetts was a source of wealth to the colony. Much of the catch was dried and shipped to foreign ports, on ships built in Massachusetts.

The authors wish to thank Walter Kossmann, whose knowledge, patience, and ability to ask all the right questions have made this a better series.

PICTURE ACKNOWLEDGMENTS

ARCHITECT OF THE CAPITOL: 10 bottom AUTHORS: 51, 53 top COLONIAL WILLIAMSBURG FOUNDATION: 6 *Harper's Weekly:* 13 bottom *Howard Pyle's Book of the American Spirit*, 1923: 24-25, 25, 26, 30-31, 45, 49 top left and top right LIBRARY COMPANY OF PHILADELPHIA: 22, 42 LIBRARY OF CONGRESS: Cover, title page, 7, 10 top, 11, 12-13, 14-15, 15 bottom, 16-17, 27, 28 bottom, 29, 32, 38, 39, 40-41, 44, 46-47, 47 top, 48 top, 48-49, 53 bottom, 54 top, 56-57, 59 NATIONAL ARCHIVES: 20, 33, 58 NATIONAL PARK SERVICE: *The Boston Mob,* copyright LOUIS S. GLANZMAN: 54-55 U.S. NAVAL ACADEMY MUSEUM, ANNAPOLIS: 50 COLLECTION OF THE NEW-YORK HISTORICAL SOCIETY: 34-35 (# 1938.312) I.N. PHELPS STOKES COLLECTION, NEW YORK PUBLIC LIBRARY: 8-9 COURTESY OF THE NORTH CAROLINA OFFICE OF ARCHIVES AND HISTORY: 21, 23 bottom, 28 top COURTESY OF THE RHODE ISLAND HISTORICAL SOCIETY: 5 and 36-37 ("The Rainbow"), 23 top (RHi X3 1575)

Contents

PROLOGUE: THE WORLD IN 1620

The year 1620, when English Pilgrims first arrived in Massachusetts, marked the beginning of England's second permanent colony in North America. The earlier surviving English colony, Virginia, had been settled since 1607 by the "gentlemen" and "adventurers" of the Virginia Company.

Europe had begun to explore the wider world during the Renaissance, a 150-year period of invention and discovery beginning in the 1400s. Advances in **navigation** and the building of better sailing ships allowed longer voyages. So began the Age of Exploration, with great navigators from Portugal, Spain, Italy, the Netherlands, France, and England sailing into uncharted waters. The explorers reached Africa, India, the Pacific Ocean, China, Japan, and Australia. They encountered kingdoms and civilizations that had existed for centuries.

The voyages from Europe to these distant shores went around Africa. This made the trip long and dangerous. So, European explorers began to sail westward in search of shortcuts. In 1492, the explorer Christopher Columbus landed on an island on the far side of the Atlantic Ocean and claimed it for Spain. He thought that he had actually sailed all the way around the world and come to an island near India. Years of exploration by numerous sailors

Spanish and French explorers led the English and Dutch in redrawing the map of the land across the Atlantic Ocean. Jacques Cartier explored Canada beginning in 1534 and tried unsuccessfully to start a colony. The French, mainly Roman Catholics, led by Samuel de Champlain, did not establish a permanent settlement in Canada until 1604. Far to the south, French Protestants had tried to start colonies in South Carolina and Florida, and been driven off by the Spaniards in 1562 and 1564. Several Frenchmen had explored inland North America, including the Mississippi valley, the Great Lakes, and Niagara Falls. The Spanish were far ahead of other Europeans in the competition for land in the Americas. Before the first English people came to America, the Spanish had already claimed huge portions of both North and South America. They had conquered two mighty Native American empires—the Aztecs and the Incas— and introduced the first domestic cattle and horses to the Americas. They founded the first two permanent cities—St. Augustine in 1565 and Santa Fe in 1610—in what would become the United States. They brought European civilization as well, including printing presses and universities. The Spanish also brought their chosen form of Christianity, Roman Catholicism, and converted hundreds of Native Americans, often by force.

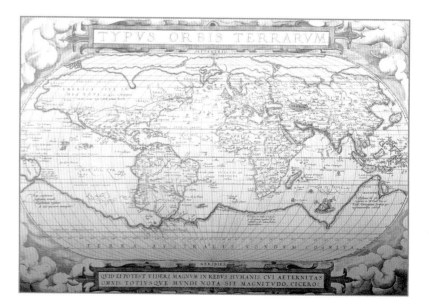

passed before the people of Europe realized that Columbus had been the first European of their era to set foot in a land unknown to them. They called this land the New World, although it was not new to the people who lived there. After Columbus, Amerigo Vespucci claimed to have reached the New World. Whether he actually did or not, in 1507 a mapmaker put his name on a map, and the New World became America, or the Americas. Still looking for a shortcut to the riches of Asia, European explorers continued to sail to North and South America. They began to claim large pieces of these lands for their own nations.

The first English ship to cross the Atlantic Ocean was commanded by the Italian-born John Cabot in 1497. Cabot's exploration of the eastern coast of Canada formed the basis for all of England's future claims to American colonies.

The first Europeans to visit Massachusetts may have been Vikings who arrived around the year 1000.

A succession of explorers reached land on the eastern coast of North America, and several of them explored the coast of Massachusetts. The Italian seaman, Giovanni da Verrazano, commanded a French expedition in 1524 and explored and charted the coast from the Carolinas to Maine. The little-known Esteban Gomez charted a portion of the New England coast for Spain the following year.

In the meantime, Walter Raleigh sponsored expeditions to America and claimed for England a large expanse of land he called Virginia. The disappearance of his last colonists from Roanoke Island some time after 1587 remains an enduring mystery.

In 1602, Englishman Bartholomew Gosnold set out to revisit the New England coast that Verrazano had charted and start a colony there. After successfully landing on the Massachusetts coast, Gosnold and his men decided they did not have enough food to survive, so they returned to England with a ship full of furs, logs, and **sassafras** roots. Gosnold was followed in 1603 by English trader Martin Pring, also in search of sassafras and other trade goods. French explorer Samuel de Champlain then spent two years charting the New England coast and searching out a site for a French colony, but hard winters and French politics conspired to defeat the effort.

Members of the Virginia Company, which had founded the colony at Jamestown, at the same time sponsored a New England colony on the coast of Maine. This colony failed because, after one winter, the settlers found life too harsh. The unsuccessful colonists returned to England in 1608. Former Virginia colonist Captain John Smith explored and mapped the coast of New England in 1614, and his description kept interest in the area alive. But New England, with its cold northern winters, needed settlers with a special kind of endurance to found a lasting colony. The **Pilgrims** and **Puritans** were the first to have such endurance.

Europe was no stranger to religious strife when English Christians began looking for a religious haven in America. For centuries in western Europe, Christianity and Roman Catholicism had been one and the same, with all Christians ruled from Rome by the Pope. But in 1517, Martin Luther, a German monk, protested some of the actions of the Roman Catholic Church. This began the **Protestant** Reformation. In 1534, the English King Henry VIII took

Captain John Smith returned from Jamestown, Virginia, to England, and then sailed again across the Atlantic to explore and map the New England coast. His book, *A Description of New England*, painted a rosy picture of Massachusetts. Smith called it a "paradise."

advantage of the Protestant Reformation. The Pope would not grant him a divorce, so he formed the Church of England and declared himself its head. The Church of England, also called the **Anglican** church, became a Protestant church, independent of the Pope but still Christian.

Then, in 1554, Queen Mary restored Catholicism as the official religion of England. She executed more than 250 people who had continued practicing Protestantism, and for this reason, people called her "Bloody Mary." Five years later, Queen Elizabeth I restored the Church of England. Under her rule, and that of the next two kings, Catholicism was outlawed, and those who continued to practice it faced arrest. Even under Protestant rule, however, many English Protestants grew dissatisfied with the Church of England. Among them were the Pilgrims and the Puritans.

For most people, life in England in the early 1600s was hard. The Stuart **dynasty** had followed the great Queen Elizabeth I to the throne. Whereas Elizabeth had been tolerant, many thought that the Stuarts acted like tyrants. Rich people had taken over much of the rural land, forcing poor people to leave the countryside and move to urban centers to search for jobs. During the first half of the century London grew by more than fifty percent. Crowded conditions made epidemics, including the terrible bubonic plague, more deadly. In 1618 the Thirty Years' War began, and this, too, caused great suffering and loss of life and property. England joined with other Protestant nations to fight Catholic powers in Spain and central Europe. Troubled people looked toward God and religion for help in such violent times. But religion, too, was a source of conflict.

DYNASTY: SERIES OF RULERS FROM THE SAME FAMILY, WHO PASS THE THRONE FROM ONE FAMILY MEMBER TO ANOTHER

I.
PLYMOUTH COLONY

THE SEPARATISTS

Men and women who called themselves Puritans complained about the Church of England, or Anglican church. They believed that this church included too many sinners. The Puritans wanted to purify the church by expelling sinners.

The Puritans also complained about many other aspects of the Anglican church. The Puritans wanted individual churches to have the power to control their own membership, and the members, in turn, to be able to control their local leaders. In this way the Puritan church would consist only of true believers. Puritans wanted to **reform** the church from within. Most English Puritans thought that the best way to accomplish their goals was to gain control of the

Above: The Separatist group that met at the home of William Brewster in England became the group we know as the Pilgrims. Brewster served as the Pilgrims' minister in the Netherlands, and then in Massachusetts.

Pilgrims praying before departing the port of Leyden, the Netherlands

government. They knew this would take time. Meanwhile, they believed that it was their Christian duty to support the church while they worked to reform it.

A much smaller group of Puritans had a different idea. They were unwilling to wait for political change. They wanted to separate themselves immediately from the corrupt and the sinners. The Anglican church responded by harassing and sometimes even killing those who promoted this idea of separation. So, some of these small separatist groups fled to the Netherlands. Among them was a group led by William Bradford that became known as the Pilgrims. In 1608 Bradford led his followers to Amsterdam. Later they moved to the port of Leyden. In 1620 Bradford took the bold step of leading his people across the Atlantic to settle in America.

THE MAYFLOWER COMPACT

Bradford and 34 other Pilgrims left the Netherlands in the spring aboard a sailing ship called the *Mayflower*. The ship entered the English port of Plymouth where about 40 more Separatists and a handful of other people boarded. The *Mayflower* departed Plymouth on September 16, 1620. It was a miserable time of year to make the 3,000-mile (4,828-kilometer) voyage across the Atlantic. Frequent storms made the passengers seasick.

The *Mayflower* spent nine weeks at sea and was blown off course from its intended destination of Virginia.

The *Mayflower* arrived at the coast of Cape Cod, Massachusetts, in late November. The Pilgrims had intended to settle much farther south, on land owned by the Virginia Company, but rough water and dangerous currents convinced them to stay at Cape Cod. Pilgrim leaders worried that some of the colonists might leave the group and settle on their own. So, they wrote an agreement, or compact, stating that they were a single group for the purpose of forming a government. The compact also said that the signers would live by the laws and regulations that the government would establish some time later. Forty-one of the male passengers signed the compact, which later became known as The Mayflower Compact.

The Pilgrims explored the nearby land along Cape Cod. When they came across some cleared fields they found stores of corn. The Pilgrims took the corn without pausing to consider that they were stealing it from someone. That someone was the Nauset Indians, who naturally took

Left: Signing the Mayflower Compact. The Mayflower Compact established the idea that a just government originates in the consent of those it is to govern. Much later, the leaders of the American Revolution used this idea when they wrote the Declaration of Independence.

Below: During the stormy and turbulent voyage, a baby, Peregrine White, was born on board the ship and slept in this crib .

Right: Two key figures in the survival of Plymouth Colony were Captain Miles Standish, the colony's military leader, and the Native American Squanto.

offense. During the next days the Nausets repeatedly attacked the Pilgrims.

The Pilgrims moved to a nearby harbor that offered shelter for their ship. A convenient hill provided a place where they could build a fort to defend themselves. The area had much clean water. The Pilgrims named this place Plymouth, the same name as the English port from which they had departed.

Now came the starving time, a long winter during which the Pilgrims struggled to survive. They took shelter on land in crude lean-tos or in cellars dug into the earth. Many stayed aboard the *Mayflower*. William Bradford wrote that at one time only six or seven people—including the **militia** captain, Miles Standish, and the minister, William Brewster—were strong enough to care for all the others: they "fetched them wood, made them fires, dressed them meat, made their beds, washed their loathsome clothes, clothed and unclothed them." By the time spring arrived about half of the original colonists were dead.

In March, the Wampanoag leader, Massasoit, visited Plymouth. Massasoit signed a treaty with the Pilgrims that promised friendly relations between the two groups. The treaty worked because each side wanted something from the other. The Pilgrims wanted the land. The Wampanoags

MILITIA: GROUP OF CITIZENS NOT NORMALLY PART OF THE ARMY WHO JOIN TOGETHER TO DEFEND THEIR LAND IN AN EMERGENCY

Below: Plymouth in 1622. The Pilgrims struggled to be self-sufficient. In 1631 a colonist wrote to his parents back in England, "we do not know how long we may subsist, for we cannot live here without provisions from Old England."

wanted help against their bitter enemies the Narra-gansetts. The treaty held for more than 50 years.

During the first summer, an orphaned Native American named Squanto lived with the Pilgrims. Squanto taught the Pilgrims many things they needed to know, including how to grow crops and where to hunt and fish. In the fall, Squanto guided the Pilgrims to what would become Boston harbor. Here the Pilgrims traded with Massachuset Indians.

The Pilgrims harvested their first crop in the autumn of 1621. After living in their new homes for one year, they decided to celebrate their good fortune with a feast of thanksgiving.

The Pilgrims celebrate a thanksgiving. This legendary celebration became the basis for the modern Thanksgiving holiday. The first Thanksgiving took place some time in the autumn of 1621 after the harvest was completed. The entire colony plus Massasoit and about 90 Native Americans feasted together for almost a week. The native peoples shot several deer for the feast, and Pilgrims shot wild fowl. It is not known whether any of these wild fowl were turkeys. For entertainment, the men competed at target shooting, or according to one Pilgrim, "exercised our arms."

2.
MASSACHUSETTS IN 1620

PHYSICAL FEATURES

The neat orange lines on the map are somewhat misleading. In fact, Massachusetts was a mix of zones featuring great variety. A single hillside might have white and black oaks on the crest, chestnut and birch in the middle slopes, and tulip poplar, beech, and hemlock in the valley below. Each of these different mixes of trees created a different habitat.

Great glaciers formed the physical landscape of Massachusetts. Glaciers carved out a jagged coastline and scoured the Coastal Plain, leaving a thin layer of soil and numerous areas of rock. The Coastal Plain is between 30 and 50 miles wide. West of the Coastal Plain is the Upland Region, a region of rolling plains. Here, in central Massachusetts are numerous rivers, ponds, and lakes. When the glaciers retreated north, they left behind large rocks that dot the Upland Region. The land rises in the west up to 1,000 feet (305 meters) above sea level and then descends into the valley created by the Connecticut River. This river's wide flood plain has some of the most fertile soil in all of Massachusetts. West of the Connecticut River

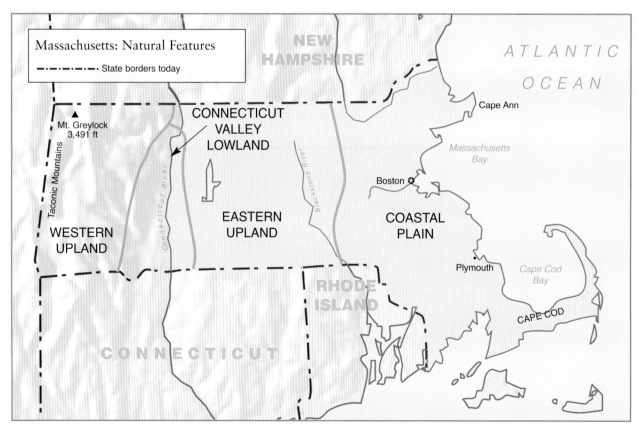

are the Berkshire Hills and Taconic Mountains. The highest point, Mount Greylock, rises 3,491 feet (1,064 meters) and is located in the state's northwest corner.

Winters are cold in Massachusetts. Spring typically comes slowly. Summers are warm and autumn lingers for an especially long time. The hottest month is July, with an average temperature of 71°F (21°C). The coolest is January with an average temperature of 26°F (-3°C). The Atlantic Ocean makes the coast warmer than inland areas. On average, the entire state receives more than 40 inches (101 centimeters) of rainfall per year, enough moisture to support agriculture. The higher, colder, inland areas receive much of this water in the form of snow. The southeast part of Massachusetts enjoys a growing season nearly six months long. In the western hills and mountains, the growing season is two months shorter.

Cape Cod, site of the first permanent English settlement, has the mildest climate in all of New England. On average, 44 inches of rain fall and there are more than 210 frost-free days. This combination was fortunate for the first colonists. In 1620, enormous schools of fish inhabited the coastal waters off Massachusetts.

A lighthouse stands guard over the Massachusetts coast at Cape Cod, a favorite destination for tourists for many years. Some parts of the Massachusetts coast have sandy beaches, but the coast becomes rocky north of Boston at Cape Ann.

Birch trees are common in the higher, cooler parts of Massachusetts. This region once featured a tremendous variety of trees. English colonists, who were used to a land stripped nearly bare of tall trees, saw great commercial potential in the colony's forests.

Cape Cod received its name because of the codfish, but there were also great schools of other fin fish, including haddock, herring, tuna, swordfish, and flounder. Lobsters and clams were common.

Like the other North American colonies, Massachusetts was mostly covered by forest. The type of vegetation depended upon average temperatures and soil conditions. The sandy coast had pitch pine and scrub oak. The dunes provided shelter for beech plum and rose hips. As the land rose, hardwoods such as oak, chestnut, and maple dominated. However, there were also large stands of softwoods—white pine, tamarack, hemlock— particularly in the northern and central parts of the colony. On the colony's higher, western slopes, sugar maple, yellow birch, beech, white pine, and hemlock thrived. The highest elevations supported red spruce and balsam fir.

THE NATIVE PEOPLES OF MASSACHUSETTS

The colony received its name from the Massachuset Native Americans. The word Massachuset means "at the range of hills" and refers to the high ground around what became Milton. The Massachuset Native Americans, like the other tribes living in the colony, belonged to the Algonquian linguistic family. The Algonquian were hunters, gatherers, and farmers. About 7,000 Native Americans lived in Massachusetts at the time the first English settlers arrived.

In order to survive, the native peoples had learned how

Native Americans fished the bountiful coastal waters.

SACHEM: ALGONQUIAN WORD FOR CHIEF

The Algonquian Indians made beads, called wampum, from the white shell of the conch or whelk (clam) and the purple segments of the quahog shell. Strings and belts of such beads served many uses, as currency, decorations or gifts, or to confirm public agreements.

to cope with New England's dramatic seasonal changes. They lived in small villages to reduce the strain on available natural resources. These villages were not permanent. Instead, the Algonquians moved with the seasons. During the winter, animals were easier to track and hunt, so the Native Americans mostly ate meat. In spring they moved to coastal areas where the men cleared fields using hatchets to slash through the bark and kill the trees and fire to burn away the underbrush. The women then became farmers for the season, planting corn, squash, and beans between the tree stumps. They fertilized their crops with fish. After the harvest in the early autumn, the tribe moved inland again to find winter quarters.

Survival during the winter was hard. Families depended on the hunting skills of the father to provide food. The father was very much the head of the family. Women did a great deal of work, but the man was always the boss. However, the women retained all property rights. Boys received training to become hunters and warriors.

The Algonquians lived without much government. Men held the political authority. When small arguments arose, a leader and his council of elders settled things. Larger decisions involving entire villages were made by calling a meeting, or powwow. Powwows often lasted for several days before reaching a decision. Each community was part of a tribe and each tribe had its own top leader, or grand **sachem**. The grand sachems made the weighty decisions regarding war or peace.

Before the Europeans arrived, the Algonquians often fought wars among themselves. The wars were usually about control of territory. The goal was to capture the enemy camp and take prisoners. The fortunate prisoners were adopted into the tribe, while the others had to endure terrible torture before they were killed.

3.
MASSACHUSETTS BAY COLONY

In the years after the founding of Plymouth Colony, new English settlements sprang up in Massachusetts. Some proved failures and were abandoned while others prospered and grew. The first settlers understood that survival depended upon receiving supplies from Europe. So, they located their villages beside good natural harbors such as Salem and Boston.

Initially the settlers found timber close at hand. Later they looked inland where they saw vast forests offering tempting timber supplies. The best way to move goods and supplies was along the rivers. Moreover, the rivers provided freshwater fishing for Atlantic salmon, sturgeon, and shad. Finally, the soils along the river were rich in nutrients and thus offered the best farming. So the river valleys became the highways along which the colonists began moving inland.

In 1630, John Winthrop and about 1,000 Puritans came to Massachusetts to settle around Boston Bay. They came with their own **charter** and called their new land the Massachusetts Bay Colony. Unlike the Pilgrims, Winthrop's colonists enjoyed financial backing and came with many supplies. They quickly occupied the best sites

The London investors in the Massachusetts Bay Company unanimously chose John Winthrop to govern the colony. Winthrop accepted because he believed he could better help purify the church in America than in England. Winthrop expected his Puritan colony to be an example to the world, writing, "We shall be a city upon a hill, the eyes of all people upon us."

Even with financial backing from England, about one in five Puritan colonists died from malnutrition and disease during their first winter in Massachusetts.

Below: Puritan leaders controlled many aspects of life in the colony. They saw it as everyone's duty to watch their neighbors for signs of sinful behavior. They also believed that all religious holidays should be treated with solemnity, and any form of gaiety on Christmas was forbidden by law. In this image, a Puritan governor interrupts Christmas festivities.

Right: The Puritans expelled from their colony people who believed in other religions. They especially objected to Quakers who tried to spread their beliefs by speaking out in public.

and set to work planting crops. Under Governor Winthrop's leadership, the Puritans organized an efficient government that included courts, police, and tax collectors. Still, the Puritans' first winter was hard.

The Puritans believed that only devout churchgoers were suitable for leadership positions in their colony. They discriminated against nonbelievers. They also believed that the Massachusetts Bay Colony could quickly grow to become independent from all English authority. The Puritan leaders were self-confident to the point of arrogance.

By 1640 there were about 300 well-educated Puritan clergymen living in Bay Colony. They worked hard to

ORTHODOXY: TRADITIONAL SET OF BELIEFS CONSIDERED BY THE AUTHORITIES TO BE CORRECT

BANISH: TO EXPEL A CITIZEN FROM HIS OR HER COUNTRY

Anne Hutchinson had many followers when she was banished from Massachusetts. She lived in Rhode Island until her husband's death, then moved with family and friends to Dutch-controlled Long Island in 1642. The following year, Hutchinson and others were killed by Indians in revenge for the Dutch governor's massacre of a defenseless Indian village.

promote Puritan religious ideas. A religion that had been founded on the basis of separation from the established, or orthodox, views of the Anglican church became the new **orthodoxy**. As such, the Puritans did not tolerate people who disagreed with them.

A series of challenges began in the mid-1630s. Reverend Roger Williams had come to Massachusetts with the first wave of Puritans in 1630. He was well respected until he started preaching that the General Court of the Bay Colony, which served as the colony's legislature, did not have authority to **act** in religious matters. Williams demanded the total separation of church and state. The General Court **banished** Williams from the colony in 1635, and he traveled southward to found a new colony at Providence, Rhode Island.

The next year, a very devout woman named Anne

When Harvard College was established in 1636, all students were required to understand Latin because all subjects were taught in Latin. Massachusetts had a well-educated population. The government of Massachusetts promoted public education by opening a public secondary school in Boston in 1635. By the 1640s, any town with 50 households was required to support a public elementary school.

Hutchinson began saying many of the same things that Williams had said. However, Hutchinson went further, saying that she had the direct word of God on matters of religious doctrine. The Puritans viewed Hutchinson's words as **heresy.** She, too, was banished and moved to Rhode Island.

The important result of these and other religious battles was that the Puritans defined the relationship between church and state in the Bay Colony. This relationship was something new, something the Puritans called "The New England Way." The Puritans made sure that the New England Way, the new orthodoxy, would endure by founding Harvard College in 1636. Young clergymen would be trained in the New England Way while attending Harvard and then would go out to the community to promote the new orthodoxy.

Above: By modern standards, punishments for crime were severe. However, the death sentence was reserved for major crimes such as murder, witchcraft, and armed rebellion. People were confined to the stocks, a form of public humiliation, for minor crimes.

Puritan control of the Massachusetts Bay Colony extended into many aspects of life. The General Court set wages and prices of merchandise. It made rules about how to dress and told people where they could live. The goal of such laws was to create a stable Christian society that remained true to Puritan ideals. The effort pleased the most devout Puritans. It made life uncomfortable for almost everyone else. Increasing numbers of colonists began to view the Puritan laws as too restrictive.

Slowly the religious leaders lost control. When the colonists had to struggle for survival, they accepted strict religious control. Once the colonists became established, people did not need to cooperate so much. They wanted to pursue personal ambitions including buying more land and making more

Opposite Bottom: A wedding in Plymouth Colony. Although most Puritan men and about half of the women knew how to read, Puritan women were expected to obey their husbands and devote themselves to household duties. Governor Winthrop wrote of a woman who had lost "her understanding and reason" because she devoted "herself wholly to reading and writing," and meddled "in such things as are proper for men, whose minds are stronger."

Below: Puritans walk to church, the men carrying guns to protect against Indians. Puritan churches came to be called Congregationalist churches because each congregation made its own decisions.

money. Winthrop complained that "self-love" had grown strong and "how little public spirit appeared in the country."

The same problems were occurring at Plymouth. By the 1640s, the great Pilgrim leader, William Bradford, saw that his vision of a religious community was fading. Many Plymouth settlers left the old village to settle elsewhere. Bradford sadly noted how the "poor" Pilgrim church was left, "like an ancient mother grown old and forsaken of her children."

The first colonial leaders had imposed the ideal of the common good that eventually would lead to personal salvation. By the 1650s, colonists remained interested in the common good. However, many now focused on material wealth and personal well-being.

4.
COLONIAL LIFE IN MASSACHUSETTS

The first settlers lived in primitive conditions. Their homes were crude dugouts carved from the earth, Indian-style wigwams, or simple cabins made of woven sticks and clay. When settlers became more established, they built small simple one-room homes. A typical home measured perhaps twenty feet long by sixteen feet wide. Ideally, they located their homes atop a gentle rise so water would drain away and they could dig a dry cellar to store food for the winter. A large stone fireplace and chimney stood at one end. It provided heat and served as a baking oven. A simple stairway led to the upstairs sleeping area.

Most colonists were farmers. Historians estimate that more than 90 percent of colonists made a living from the land. In Massachusetts, the colonial leaders made treaties with the Native Americans to purchase the land, and then granted plots to individual colonists. Clearing land to allow farming was hard work. Farmers had to cut down trees and remove the stumps. Then they dug out the rocks. They used **oxen** to pull a heavy plow through the soil to prepare it for planting. The first crops were usually corn, wheat, and rye. Meanwhile, the farmer's wife maintained a kitchen garden where she grew seasonal vegetables such as cabbage and beans.

The wife and children raised chickens, ducks, and geese for eggs and meat. A dairy cow was a luxury, oxen a necessity, a horse very useful if it could be afforded. Most farmers kept pigs because they could run wild and fend for themselves during the warm months. If a farmer had enough land, he could also graze cattle and plant an orchard.

The dugout offered the advantage of allowing newly arrived colonists to put a roof over their heads as quickly as possible.

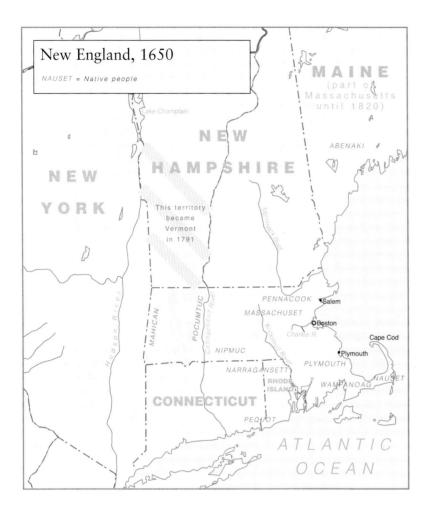

New England, 1650

NAUSET = Native people

MAINE
(part of
Massachusetts
until 1820)

NEW
HAMPSHIRE

Lake Champlain

ABENAKI

NEW
YORK

This territory
became
Vermont
in 1791

Merrimack River

Hudson River

MAHICAN

POCUMTUC

Connecticut River

PENNACOOK

Salem

MASSACHUSET

N. Charles River

Boston

Charles R.

NIPMUC

Cape Cod

PLYMOUTH

Plymouth

NARRAGANSETT

RHODE
ISLAND

WAMPANOAG

NAUSET

CONNECTICUT

PEQUOT

ATLANTIC
OCEAN

With the help of neighbors, a one-room house could be built in a few days.

Above: The fireplace provided heat, light, and a place to cook. It was the gathering place of the colonial home.

IMPORT: TO BRING MERCHANDISE INTO THE COUNTRY FOR SALE; MERCHANDISE BROUGHT INTO THE COUNTRY

WEST INDIES: ISLANDS OF THE CARIBBEAN SEA, SO CALLED BECAUSE THE FIRST EUROPEAN VISITORS THOUGHT THEY WERE NEAR INDIA

During the colonial era, most farmers were poor. They had to work very hard simply for their families to survive from one year to the next. Their lifetime goal was to hand over their farms to the children with the hope that their children would enjoy a better life.

As the years passed, conditions did improve. Many farmers were able to grow more than their families needed. They sold the extra, or surplus, to merchants. The merchants, in turn, exported the surplus from the port of Boston to distant places, particularly the **West Indies** and Europe. The merchants used their profits to purchase goods to **import** back to Massachusetts. To complete the circle, successful farmers bought imports such as better tools to farm more efficiently or perhaps luxury items like fine dishes or nice clothes. People could make money if they worked hard and were fortunate.

Massachusetts Printers

Almost 200 years passed between the invention of the printing press in Germany and 1640 when a printing press first operated in England's American colonies. The first printing press was in Cambridge, Massachusetts. The press's first book was the Bay Psalm Book. Before long, numerous printers practiced their trade in the Boston area. The Puritan population was highly literate and demanded reading materials, mostly about religion. The printing business expanded rapidly, and Boston area printers turned out hundreds of pamphlets containing religious tracts, arguments, sermons, prayers, and hymns.

Demand grew also for literature and almanacs. The poetry of Anne Bradstreet, who had arrived in Massachusetts at the age of eighteen, and Mary Rowlandson's story of her captivity among the Indians, A Narrative of the Captivity and Restoration of Mrs. Mary Rowlandson, were both published in Boston. Boston became a publishing center, which it remains today. Many colonial printers learned their trade in Boston. The most notable of these was Benjamin Franklin. Having learned the printer's trade from his brother, Franklin left Boston at the age of seventeen and went to work in Philadelphia, where he became America's best-known colonial publisher.

The first newspaper in the American colonies, the News-Letter, began publication in Boston in 1704. Soon Boston printers were turning out as many as four different weekly newspapers, and several other Massachusetts' towns—Cambridge, Newburyport, Salem, and Worcester—had newspapers of their own. Newspaper publishers typically printed several hundred copies of each issue, and each copy was passed among many readers.

Colonial America's best-known printer, Benjamin Franklin, was born in Boston and learned his trade there from his older brother. He left after an argument when he was seventeen years old and moved to Philadelphia.

The Ocean and the Forest

While the majority of people worked as farmers, some people turned to the ocean for their livelihood. Oddly, the Plymouth Pilgrims did not use their prime location to exploit the ocean. However, the Puritans did. Their original charter gave them fishing rights in nearby coastal waters. Among the first colonists who came with

Abundant fishing off the coast of Massachusetts was a source of wealth to the colony. Much of the catch was dried and shipped to foreign ports on ships built in Massachusetts.

Governor Winthrop were fishermen and shipwrights. Some of the first transport ships brought materials needed to built fishing boats. In addition, there were small fishing villages around Cape Ann established by independent non-Puritan groups of English settlers.

Initially, Massachusetts fishermen stayed close to shore to fish for mackerel, haddock, and pollack. In 1640, revolution in England prevented English fishermen from

sailing to New England waters. Their absence opened the door for Massachusetts fishermen. From this date forward, fishing in Massachusetts increased rapidly. More was caught than could be eaten in Massachusetts, so gradually fishermen expanded their market by selling salted or dried fish to the other colonies, the Caribbean, southern Europe, and England.

Massachusetts fishermen became a tough and independent group. In 1644, the fishing port Marblehead did not have a single church member. Seventy-five years later, a newly arrived minister complained that the port's fishermen were "as rude, swearing, drunken, and fighting a crew as they were poor."

While Massachusetts fishermen turned east to harvest the sea, other people went west to harvest the rivers and forests. Initially, traders hoped to trade with the Native

Hand-sawing lumber with a two-man saw. The man in the saw pit had the dirtiest job because sawdust fell and stuck to his sweat-soaked skin.

Americans to obtain valuable furs. But western Massachusetts did not support a commercially successful fur trade. However, it did support a profitable timber business.

Massachusetts merchants hired workers to fell trees, build sawmills, and manufacture wood products. For example, the Hutchinson family in Boston owned nineteen sawmills in New Hampshire. New Hampshire wood products such as barrel **staves** and shingles were exported both to the other colonies and to the West Indies.

Giant white pine trees proved the most profitable. The Royal Navy had a great and continuing need for trees suitable to make masts for sailing ships. A single mast tree exported to England was worth a great deal of money.

Farming, fishing, and timber all provided valuable exports. They gave rise to an increasingly powerful class of merchants, most of whom lived in Boston. Boston merchant families established trade relationships throughout the Atlantic. The West Indies were a particularly profitable market. As early as 1647, Governor John Winthrop noted that West Indian **planters** were "so intent upon planting sugar that they had rather buy food at very dear rates than produce it" themselves. Massachusetts merchants were quite happy to sell to these planters dried fish and grain as well as wood to build plantations, horses and cattle to power sugar mills, and staves to make sugar barrels. Massachusetts trading ships also sailed to Africa to purchase slaves, and then sold the slaves in the West Indies.

Overall, prosperity in Massachusetts depended on seaborne trade, which became ever more important to the colony's economy. The farming and fishing communities in eastern Massachusetts gradually changed to become busy seaports.

Plymouth grew to become a thriving town with spacious houses and tree-lined streets.

PLANTER: OWNER OF A PLANTATION, OR LARGE FARM

STAVE: STRIP OF WOOD USED TO MAKE BARRELS

5.
A GROWING POPULATION LEADS TO WAR

The Massachusetts Bay Colony grew rapidly. By 1635, about 2,000 immigrants were coming to the colony each year and most of them were Puritans. The newcomers settled all along the Atlantic coast from Maine, which at this time was part of Massachusetts, to Long Island. They also spread inland up the major rivers to found new towns as far west as Springfield. They ignored Dutch claims to Connecticut and founded towns at Hartford and nearby Wethersfield and Windsor. However, they could not ignore the Native American who lived on the land they settled.

THE PEQUOT WAR

The Pequot Indians lived in Connecticut. When they objected to the English invasion, the English prepared to

Town Meetings

Local government authority in New England rested in each town or village. The town meeting became the forum in which townsmen elected their leaders and voted on everything from land distribution and taxation to what to do about stray animals. At first, only free Puritan men who were church members were allowed to participate in town meetings. Eventually the vote was extended to all freemen who owned property. Town meetings gave the citizens some control over the way their towns were run, but many voters went along with the decisions of the wealthiest and most prominent local leaders. The town meetings also gave townspeople the chance to socialize and share ideas.

Any attempt to interfere with town meetings caused an uproar. When King James II placed the New England colonies under a royal governor, the governor earned widespread hatred by limiting town meetings to one a year. Just before the American Revolution, Great Britain took over Massachusetts and outlawed town meetings altogether, but this did not stop people from meeting and making decisions.

destroy them. The English made a surprise attack against the main Pequot village in 1637. They set the village on fire and then killed everyone who tried to flee from the flames. No one knows for certain, but probably 700 Pequot men, women, and children died in just 30 minutes. After the slaughter, John Winthrop Jr. directed the English to occupy the Pequot lands.

As the population of Massachusetts spread inland, the central authority began to lose control. Puritans who attended a church far from Boston did not necessarily want to worship in exactly the same way Boston Puritans worshiped. Congregations and towns made decisions independently. Congregations managed their own affairs and selected their own clergy. Government authority seldom entered the picture, usually only to soothe disputes or to acknowledge decisions that had already been made.

Towns behaved in the same way. Without outside supervision, towns held elections, collected taxes, built roads and bridges. Towns even raised and trained their own military forces, the town militia. These military forces faced a great challenge when war broke out in 1675.

A New England town meeting. The right to vote on town decisions was limited to so-called "freemen." Freemen excluded not only slaves, but also indentured servants, who promised to work to repay their travel costs. About one colonist in three arrived in New England as an indentured servant.

KING PHILIP'S WAR

As ever-increasing numbers of English colonists came to Massachusetts, the Native Americans saw that their own way of life was in peril. White settlements surrounded many Native American villages. As the colonists cleared woodlands to create farms, Native American hunters had to travel ever farther to find wild game. A few Puritans worked hard to convert the Native Americans to Christianity. By 1675, about 1,100 native people had converted. They lived in fourteen so-called "praying villages." Here they managed their own civil affairs. Their children received free admission to elementary schools. How this experiment with whites and Native Americans living in peace would have worked out is impossible to predict because in 1675 a terrible war interrupted the lives of all the inhabitants of Massachusetts.

The Wampanoag Indians had lived in peace with the English ever since 1620 when their leader, Massasoit, made a treaty of friendship with the Pilgrims. Massasoit's son, Metacom, called King Philip by the English, saw that he was losing control of his lands and his power. Metacom organized a Native American confederacy to resist English expansion. Whether he planned to go to war against the English is unknown.

Metacom became sachem of the Wampanoags in 1662, following the death of his father, Massasoit.

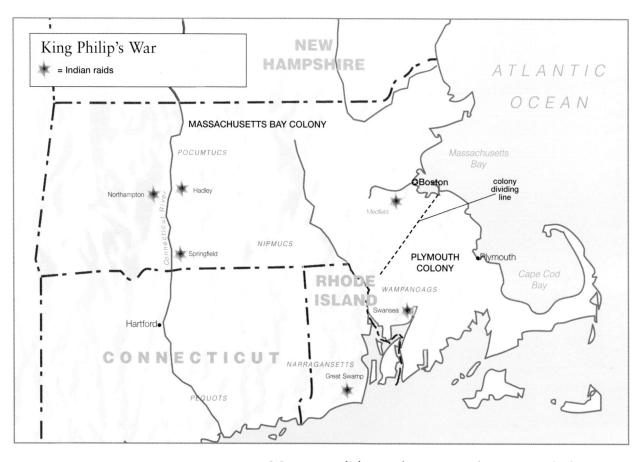

Metacom did not have complete control, however, over all the members of his tribe. In June 1675, some Wampanoag Indians attacked and burned part of the village of Swansea then in Plymouth Colony. A few days later they killed eleven Swansea men. This mass execution marked the beginning of a conflict the colonists called King Philip's War.

Plymouth Colony joined with the Bay Colony to fight King Philip. By the fall of 1675, the Narragansetts, Pocumtucs, and Nipmucs joined the Wampanoags in the battle against the English. At first the Native American enjoyed great success. They destroyed numerous villages including Springfield, Hadley, and Northampton. The native peoples made it impossible for the **frontier** villages to communicate with one another. Knowing that they were vulnerable to attack, many settlers abandoned their homes and fled east for safety.

In December, the governor of Plymouth, Josiah Winslow, led the Plymouth and Bay Colony militia in an

FRONTIER: NEWEST PLACE OF SETTLEMENT, LOCATED THE FARTHEST AWAY FROM THE CENTER OF POPULATION

Colonists preparing to defend their town during King Philip's War.

attack against Metacom's most powerful ally, the Narragansett Indians. Winslow found the Narragansetts camped on high ground in the middle of the Great Swamp. A bloody, day-long battle took place. The English lost 240 men killed and wounded, an enormous number for a battle in that era. But the Narragansetts suffered more than 900 people killed and wounded. This was more than they could endure. The English attack greatly reduced further Narragansett participation in the war.

During the winter of 1675–1676, the remaining native peoples continued to raid throughout Massachusetts. They even attacked Medfield, a town only eighteen miles west of Boston. When spring came, most Native American warriors had to concentrate on hunting and fishing in order to feed their families. The English had greater resources to support a war and so they kept hunting down the Native Americans. By June, Massachusetts leaders offered to spare any native peoples who surrendered. Hundreds of Native Americans took advantage of this offer.

All that remained was to track down Metacom himself. In August 1676, a militia captain organized a group of whites and native allies to hunt Metacom. They found and killed him on August 12, 1676. Although some fighting continued for another two years, Metacom's death marked the end of the greatest military challenge the Native Americans ever mounted against Massachusetts.

The killing of "King Philip." King Philip's War devastated New England. The war was costly in terms of both lives and property. The expansion of Plymouth and Massachusetts Colonies halted and did not fully recover for another generation.

6.
THE ENGLISH GOVERNMENT EXERTS CONTROL

Ever since the first colonists landed at Plymouth, land in New Hampshire and Maine had been part of Massachusetts. From 1641 to 1679, the Massachusetts General Court administered New Hampshire. In 1679 authorities in England gave New Hampshire to the friend of a government official, but Maine still remained part of Massachusetts.

A bigger change came about because the home country, England, wanted a colonial government that would serve the needs of English merchants. In 1676 an English official investigated Massachusetts. He reported that Massachusetts violated "all the acts of trade and navigation." This was unacceptable; so in 1684, King Charles II canceled the Massachusetts Bay Colony's charter. After King Charles' death, his brother and successor, King James II, merged all the New England colonies, plus New York and New Jersey, into the Dominion of New England under a **royal governor**, Sir Edmund Andros. In 1689, as word arrived of the unpopular King James's loss of the throne, Massachusetts citizens arrested Governor Andros and resumed control of the colony. They sent Andros back to England and appealed to the new king, William III, to restore their original charter.

At this time France and England were at war with each other in Europe, so the French in Canada and their Native American allies took advantage of the government upheaval in Massachusetts to attack the colony's frontier. In a devastating attack in 1690, the French burned an English frontier town and slaughtered dozens of men, women, and children. Rather than returning the old charter to the Puritans, the king decided to keep control of the colonial government. In 1691, England merged Plymouth Colony and the Massachusetts Bay Colony into one royal colony, Massachusetts Bay, with Boston as its capital.

Some things stayed the same. For example, the General Court still served as the legislative assembly and retained unusual power. For example, each year the General Court consulted with the royal governor to select 28 members to

Opposite: The Reverend Jonathan Edwards' most famous sermon, "Sinners in the Hands of an Angry God," contained graphic and frightening descriptions of the punishment he believed awaited sinners. Edwards served as a missionary to the Indians and eventually became the president of the College of New Jersey, the future Princeton University.

Below: A fort at Greenfield, about 1744. Forts on the western frontier were intended to protect settlers from French and Indian raids.

serve on the governor's council. In all the other colonies, the king made this choice. However, the colony's new charter demanded religious tolerance. Gone were the days when Massachusetts leaders could make their own rules. From now on, England's **Parliament** and the king held authority over Massachusetts. In spite of the new government, spiritual and social unrest in the colony gave rise to the infamous witch trials. A form of hysteria gripped the population for several years, reaching its greatest fury at Salem in 1692.

Within 100 years of the founding of Plymouth Colony, Massachusetts had changed so much that it hardly seemed like the same place. It was a prosperous colony, unified under the control of a royal governor. But some things had not changed. Most people still viewed questions about religion and morality with great seriousness. They still held a deep concern for the common good. And they still thought of themselves as different, perhaps just a little wiser and better than everyone else.

While many people devoted themselves to making money, others believed that the colony was drifting too far from its religious roots. This belief led to the revival of religious spirit, a movement called the Great Awakening. It started in Northampton where a brilliant religious thinker, Jonathan Edwards, preached about the need for people to rely on God's power to redeem themselves.

The powerful message spread across the colony. In 1740, an English **evangelist**, George Whitefield, crossed Massachusetts and converted hundreds of people from all walks of life to belief in a direct personal experience of salvation. Converts felt an intense religious spirit that turned them away from material concerns. Thousands of people gathered in Boston to listen to Whitefield's farewell sermon before he went on to the other colonies.

The Great Awakening also caused religious divisions. The converts, or "New Lights," feuded with the unconverted, or "Old Lights," about the meaning of true religion. At the same time, other people remained outside of both groups. No one completely realized it at the time, but Massachusetts had become a home for people with many different beliefs.

Witch Hunt

The witch trials in Salem and elsewhere in Massachusetts are remembered as a dark episode in American history. Mass hysteria swept through the population between 1688 and 1692. In Salem, a group of girls and young women had fits—perhaps real, perhaps fake—and accused hundreds of townspeople, usually older women, of being witches who caused their fits.

In the other towns of Massachusetts, about a hundred accused witches were tried and about a dozen executed. Of the hundreds accused in Salem in 1692, most were tried and released, but nineteen women were executed by hanging, and one man was crushed to death by boulders. As more people were accused, the population lived in terror of arrest. People made plans to leave the area. One man kept his horses saddled and armed his family so they could fight and flee if threatened with arrest. When even the governor's wife was accused, Salem's leaders finally came to their senses and put a stop to the trials. One of the judges, Samuel Sewall, was haunted by guilt and publicly apologized for his role in the witch trials.

During the 1600s, many Europeans everywhere believed in witchcraft and supernatural powers. In England and Europe, thousands of accused witches had been put to death by burning since the 1500s, but this practice had all but stopped by 1650. The Puritans, however, believed more strongly than anyone that evil was very present in the world. Some Puritan ministers saw the apparent increase in witchcraft as a punishment for the lack of religious devotion among their congregations. Other colonies had a small number of witch trials but did not put anyone to death. Any attempts to explain why the people of Salem behaved as they did can only be guesses. By the year 1700, witch trials had ceased throughout the American colonies.

Top: Reverend Cotton Mather believed in witches and witchcraft, but he also believed in science. He promoted the use of smallpox inoculations to prevent the disease.

Right: Not all people found guilty of witchcraft were executed. Those who confessed their "guilt" received other forms of punishment, such as the pictured method—being put in a pillory. Some husbands of accused women were punished for refusing to testify against their wives.

Right: Older women in Salem lived in fear of arrest during the witchcraft hysteria of 1692.

Far Right: Samuel Sewall, one of the Salem witch trial judges, five years later took responsibility for his role in the trials, stating in public that he "desires to take the blame and shame of it."

Massachusetts volunteers, commanded by Colonel William Pepperell, disembark off the Nova Scotia coast.

7.
THE FRENCH AND INDIAN WAR

England and France had a long and bitter history of rivalry and war. French colonists settled in Canada and built New France. Its capital was Quebec. French explorers claimed all of North America from the Allegheny Mountains to the Rocky Mountains and from Canada to Mexico. Few French people settled in the vast area south of Canada. Instead, French traders followed the waterways to hunt and trap and to trade with the Native American.

Great Britain and France went to war in 1740 for reasons that had nothing to do with Massachusetts. But Massachusetts people thought of themselves as patriotic citizens under the reign of the **British** king. In 1745, thousands of Massachusetts men eagerly volunteered for military duty. The Massachusetts royal governor, William Shirley, selected a **provincial** officer, William Pepperell, to lead them in an attack against the French fortress of Louisbourg.

Louisbourg stood on Cape Breton Island, at the eastern end of Nova Scotia, Canada. The fortress guarded the Gulf of St. Lawrence. Military strategists considered Louisbourg

the key to controlling Canada. Massachusetts men made up most of the 4,000-man force of New England soldiers who laid siege to the fortress. During a 55-day **campaign,** their artillery bombarded the defenders with over 9,000 cannonballs and shells. Then the French surrendered.

The capture of Louisbourg was an outstanding military victory. Massachusetts people were proud of what they had accomplished. Three years later, Britain and France made peace. As part of the peace agreement, Britain gave back Louisbourg to the French in exchange for land in India. Many Massachusetts people thought that the sacrifice had been for no purpose.

The next conflict came when British settlers began pushing across the Allegheny Mountains. As was the case in 1745, Massachusetts had nothing to do with the events that caused the conflict.

On disputed land near where modern Pittsburgh, stands, a small battle took place between Virginia militia and French soldiers. It started a long and deadly war between Great Britain and France. In Europe the war was known as the Seven Years' War. Americans called it the French and Indian War. No significant fighting took place on Massachusetts territory during this war. However, the patriotic colony supported the war both in spirit and body.

CAMPAIGN: SERIES OF ACTIONS TAKEN TO REACH A MILITARY GOAL

The fortress of Louisbourg had stone and brick walls 30-feet (9-meters) high and was armed with powerful artillery.

In 1755 the colony had a population of close to 250,000. Almost 8,000 men enlisted in provincial or regular units. This was about one man in five from the prime military ages of 16 to 29, representing a huge outpouring of patriotic zeal.

Massachusetts men fought in many of the significant campaigns during the French and Indian War. A British official praised Massachusetts as "the frontier and advanced guard of all the colonies against the enemy in Canada." The French and Indian War ended with the total defeat of the French in 1759. After France and Great Britain made peace, Canada became another British colony.

Once more Massachusetts was proud of its contribution to the victory. No one saw that the victory had brought the American Revolution closer. France had always been a common enemy of all British people in both Great Britain and in America. To fight the common enemy, the British people had united. Opposition to France had been like a glue holding the British people together. After the war, the people of Massachusetts began to see differences between themselves and the British back home.

The People of Massachusetts

Over the course of 150 years, the European population of Massachusetts grew from a few hundred to a quarter of a million. Only Pennsylvania and Virginia had greater populations. By 1770, Boston was a major colonial city with a population of 16,000, the third largest city after New York City and Philadelphia.

By the time of the Revolution, 82% of the people of Massachusetts were English. Irish and Scottish people made up about 9%, blacks about 2%, and the other 7% consisted of assorted nationalities. Few blacks lived in Massachusetts relative to other colonies. The New England soil and climate did not support large plantations, but many wealthy Boston families did have slaves as house servants.

8.
A MATTER OF TAXES

After the war ended, British leaders concluded that the American colonies had not helped as much as they should have. Moreover, the British government still needed to provide about 10,000 soldiers to defend the colonies from the Native American and from other enemies. This was a heavy expense. Never before had the British Parliament set taxes on American citizens. This changed in 1764. To help pay for the cost of defending the colonies, Parliament passed a law to raise money from the American colonies themselves.

This law was the Sugar Act. The Sugar Act imposed a tax on imports or exports. Such taxes are called duties.

Above: A replica of the British frigate *Rose*. Before the American Revolution, the *Rose* patrolled the Massachusetts coast in an effort to prevent smuggling.

Below: The port of Salem. Massachusetts towns and villages were changing dramatically from self-sufficient farming communities to more modern communities that depended on trade with the world around them. Massachusetts merchants developed trade relationships with foreign ports throughout the Atlantic.

The Sugar Act placed duties on refined sugar as well as other trade goods and provided for strict enforcement and collection procedures. The Sugar Act placed a particularly heavy burden on Massachusetts because a large part of the colony's economy depended on imports and exports. The Sugar Act was the first in a series of decisions made by the British Parliament that led to the American Revolution.

Massachusetts merchants responded to the Sugar Act by turning to **smuggling** in order to avoid paying duties. The British government, in turn, responded by trying to stop the smuggling.

When the British thought a merchant was avoiding his duties, he was sent for trial at a military court in far-away Halifax, Nova Scotia. Colonists believed that this was taking away one of their basic rights: freedom from false arrest.

Next, in 1765 Parliament passed the Stamp Act. Under the Stamp Act, colonists had to pay to have most documents stamped, or risk arrest. Even newspapers had to have stamps. The Stamp Act affected colonists of all social classes. Resistance grew throughout the colonies. Riots broke out, and groups calling themselves the Sons of Liberty attacked the offices and homes of tax collectors.

From the time of the Stamp Act until the outbreak of the Revolutionary War, conflict focused on the question of taxation and representation. Because of American opposition, Parliament repealed the Stamp Act in 1766. Americans celebrated the news. A Boston pastor spoke for many when he thanked God for saving Massachusetts "from a slavish, inglorious bondage."

Colonial leaders continued to protest what they considered unjust British rule, but they were against violence. Among the peaceful ways protesters opposed British laws was through the formation of Committees of Correspondence. By writing letters, the Committees kept one another informed and made plans for the colonies to cooperate. The Committees got all the colonies except New Hampshire to **boycott** English merchandise. The boycott convinced the British to repeal most taxes by 1770.

Five years of peaceful protest came to a sudden end. There had been many past quarrels between civilians and

Opposite: Thomas Hutchinson was the great-great-grandson of the banished heretic Anne Hutchinson. As the colony's royal governor, he became the symbol of the forces that Massachusetts protesters most despised.

British soldiers living in Boston. On March 5, 1770, a group of British soldiers went looking for trouble. In response, a crowd of Boston civilians turned out. They began to harass a British soldier who stood guard at the Customs House. A small unit of British soldiers marched to help this soldier. The crowd pelted the soldiers with rocks and garbage. The soldiers responded by firing their muskets and killing five civilians. Among the dead was Crispus Attucks, a former slave. By the next day, protesters in Boston were calling this incident a "massacre." Forever after, the incident became known as the Boston Massacre.

Boston people clamored for a trial to charge the British soldiers with murder. Few Boston lawyers wanted to

defend the soldiers. Samuel Adams was a prominent protester against British rule. But he and many other protest leaders did not want the supporters of British rule to be able to claim that Boston had fallen to mob rule. So when John Adams, Samuel's cousin, and Josiah Quincy Jr., offered to defend the soldiers, Samuel Adams said to go ahead.

The subsequent trial convicted two soldiers of manslaughter. They received the punishment of being branded on the hand. Everyone, except perhaps the two soldiers, believed that justice had been served. Boston had shown itself to be a place committed to constitutional principles of justice. Still, Boston **patriots**, people who opposed the royal government, gathered on several succeeding anniversaries of the Boston Massacre to warn against the unchecked powers of the British government.

Governor Hutchinson enjoyed all the privileges that came from being loyal to British authority. Hutchinson owned a splendid mansion full of rich furnishings. In addition to being governor, he held three judgeships and a council seat. In August 1765, during the Stamp Act riots, a mob looted Hutchinson's home.

9.
FROM BOYCOTT TO BATTLEFIELD

After 1770, Massachusetts patriots saw every action taken by the British government as a plot to take away American liberty. Nonetheless, Massachusetts prospered and colonial life remained calm until 1773. Few colonists really wanted independence from Great Britain, as long as they could make their own laws and set their own taxes. Then Parliament passed a law that gave one British tea seller, the struggling East India Company, special treatment. The East India Company was given a monopoly in the colonies so that it could sell its tea more cheaply than any other dealer. Once again, the Committees of Correspondence went to work to spread the word about the new law. The Sons of Liberty also organized actions against tea shipments.

The first such action was the famous Boston Tea Party. On December 16, 1773, a group of about 150 patriots disguised as Mohawk Native Americans dumped a large, valuable shipment of tea into Boston Harbor. Their action shocked Thomas Hutchinson, who had risen to the position of royal governor. John Adams and other patriots were pleased.

Many people in Massachusetts did not approve of the Boston Tea Party. One hundred and twenty-three Boston merchants wrote a letter to the British king, George III, telling him that they opposed this type of mob violence. This soothing letter had little impact. British leaders concluded that America was being controlled by a violent mob of radicals.

Great Britain responded to the Boston Tea Party by closing the port of Boston and placing Massachusetts under military rule. The British goal was to teach all the colonies to submit to British rule, but Boston, the main source of trouble, was the special British target. Patriots throughout the American colonies called the various British laws the Coercive Acts (also called the Intolerable Acts). Increasing numbers of people argued that they would have to fight for independence from Great Britain.

Massachusetts patriots decided to respond to the British actions by boycotting British trade. They knew that the

Below: The port of Boston before the Revolution

Above: The Boston Tea Party. John Adams understood the significance of the event. He wrote, "The People have passed the River and cut away the Bridge...This is the grandest Event, which has ever yet happened."

boycott had to involve all the colonies to be effective. They decided not to act until American leaders gathered in a congress of the colonies to discuss what to do. In the meantime, Massachusetts militia began to organize and train harder and towns began to stockpile military supplies.

The First Continental Congress took place in Philadelphia in September 1774. Among the Massachusetts delegates were Samuel and John Adams. One day Paul Revere, a rider for the Massachusetts Committee of Correspondence, brought dramatic news. Revere reported that there had been a town meeting in Suffolk County, Massachusetts, where the delegates produced a written statement called "the Suffolk Resolves."

The president of the Continental Congress read aloud the Suffolk Resolves. The Suffolk Resolves claimed that the Coercive Acts were unconstitutional and should not be obeyed. Instead, Americans should form their own government and collect their own taxes. They would not give the money to the royal authorities until Parliament repealed the Coercive Acts.

Delegates applauded and cheered. The First Continental Congress endorsed the Suffolk Resolves and drew up a set of resolutions. These resolutions set forth basic rights to life, liberty, property, and the rights of colonial assemblies to tax and make local laws. Finally, the delegates agreed to meet again in May 1775.

The First Continental Congress moved the American quarrel with Great Britain beyond just taxes. In addition to tax questions, the congress questioned whether Parliament had the right to make laws for America. The delegates agreed to end all imports from Great Britain in order to pressure Parliament to accept their views. They formed a Continental Association by which every village, town, and city was to elect a committee to enforce the decrees of the Continental Congress.

FIRST SHOTS

During the winter of 1774-1775, the Provincial Congress of Massachusetts continued to meet even though this was illegal according to the recent British law against town meetings. Massachusetts militia continued to train. A special group of militia was formed. They were named

"Minutemen" because they could answer the call to arms within a matter of minutes.

General Thomas Gage, the colony's royal governor, had instructions to enforce the Acts of Parliament and, if possible, to arrest Samuel Adams and the president of the Provincial Congress, John Hancock. Gage knew that the Massachusetts militia had gathered weapons and supplies at Concord, eighteen miles west of Boston. He organized a military force to march first to Lexington and then on to Concord to seize these items.

The British forces entered Lexington early on the morning of April 19, 1775. A small force of Minutemen stood on the Lexington Common. Which side fired the first shot is unknown. By the time the smoke cleared, eight Minutemen lay dead. Only one **redcoat** received a light wound. The Revolutionary War had begun.

American forces blockaded Boston. The British continued on to Concord to search for hidden weapons and supplies. Meanwhile, American militia gathered from nearby towns. Fighting broke out and continued for the remainder of the day as the British retreated back to Boston. On June 16, the Americans began to fortify a hill overlooking Boston harbor. The next day the British attacked them. The bloody Battle of Bunker Hill convinced both American rebels and British political leaders that war was inevitable.

Two weeks later, General George Washington arrived to take command of the American forces outside of Boston. On March 17, 1776, after an eleven-month siege, the British evacuated the city. No additional significant fighting took place on Massachusetts soil for the remainder of the Revolutionary War. However, Massachusetts soldiers and politicians played vital roles during the war.

The revolutionary government of Massachusetts began work on a state constitution in 1777. A long period of discussion and rewriting followed, as the towns met and commented on each draft. A draft written by John Adams, Samuel Adams, and James Bowdoin finally received approval on June 16, 1780. Massachusetts became the sixth state to approve the United States Constitution on February 6, 1788.

Opposite: Several hundred whaling ships operated from Massachusetts seaports during the height of the whaling industry in the 1800s.

John Adams, a prominent Massachusetts delegate at the First Continental Congress and a future president of the United States. When the Congress voted to support the Massachusetts patriots, Adams wrote that it was "one of the happiest Days of my Life … . This Day convinced me that America will support Massachusetts or perish with her."

EPILOGUE

Modern Massachusetts has more than six million people, half of whom live in or around the state capital, Boston. The state's next largest cities are Worcester and Springfield. During the 1800s, many immigrants came from Ireland and other parts of Europe to work in the state's cotton mills and factories. Ninety percent of the state population is of European descent. About five percent of the population is black. Fewer than one percent of the people are Native American, most of whom live on Cape Cod. The rest of the population is divided among Hispanic Americans, Asian Americans, French Canadians, and others. Massachusetts was first settled by Protestants who did not tolerate other religions, but today much of the population is Roman Catholic.

Although Massachusetts was dominated by agriculture during colonial times, today only one percent of the state economy is based on agriculture. Close to half of the nation's cranberries are grown on Cape Cod. During the 1820s, a group of businessmen built Lowell as a planned factory town. The booming textile industry transformed the Massachusetts economy. Although many of the factories eventually closed, manufacturing today employs about twenty-two percent of the state's workers, with computer parts and electrical equipment as major products. Massachusetts is a center of technological research and development, medical research, the fine arts, and education. Harvard has been joined by numerous other well-respected colleges and universities.

Massachusetts has long led the nation's fishing industry. Cape Cod had received its name in 1602, from the English trader, Bartholomew Gosnold, for the abundant codfish in the surrounding waters. During the 1800s, whaling ships sailed from Massachusetts ports. Relentless overfishing has nearly wiped out the populations of many fish species, and is destroying the fishing industry.

Gosnold also named the island, Martha's Vineyard, after his daughter. Although codfish are nearly gone from Massachusetts waters, Cape Cod, Martha's Vineyard, Cape Ann, Nantucket, and other coastal areas attract numerous summer visitors to their beaches.

Massachusetts offers many sites where visitors can learn about colonial and Revolutionary history. A full-size replica of the Mayflower and the re-created settlement of Plimoth Plantation can be seen at Plymouth. Salem offers the Salem Witch Museum and the recreated 1630 settlement, Pioneer Village. Boston's Freedom Trail provides a walking tour of colonial and Revolutionary sites, and the first battle of the Revolution is commemorated at the Minuteman National Historic Park in Concord.

DATELINE

1524: Giovanni da Verrazano explores the coast of New England.

1602: Bartholomew Gosnold leads a failed attempt to establish a colony on an island off the coast of Massachusetts. While there, he names Cape Cod and Martha's Vineyard.

1607–1608: A group of English colonists spend the winter on the coast of Maine (part of Massachusetts until 1820), but give up and return to England.

1608: Pilgrims move from England to the Netherlands.

1614: Captain John Smith explores and maps the New England coast. His book about his voyage promotes interest in the area as a potential colony.

1620: The Pilgrims sail on the *Mayflower* from the Netherlands to Massachusetts, and found a colony at Plymouth.

1630: Puritans from England establish the Massachusetts Bay Colony.

1635: Roger Williams is banished from Massachusetts for his beliefs and leads his followers to Rhode Island.

1636: Anne Hutchinson is banished for her beliefs and goes to Rhode Island. Harvard College is established. Thomas Hooker leads his congregation to settle in Connecticut. Massachusetts colonists slaughter hundreds of Pequot Indians and take over their land.

1675–1676: King Philip's War, between the colonists and the Wampanoag Native Americans, results in the Native Americans' defeat and the death of their chief, King Philip.

1680: New Hampshire is separated from Massachusetts.

1684: The king of England cancels Massachusetts's colonial charter, making Massachusetts a royal colony.

MARCH 5, 1770: A confrontation between Boston civilians and British soldiers ends in the shooting deaths of five civilians. Patriots call the incident the "Boston Massacre."

DECEMBER 16, 1773: In a protest known as the "Boston Tea Party," Bostonians dressed as Native Americans board British trading ships and dump a large cargo of tea into Boston Harbor.

APRIL 19, 1775: The first battle of the American Revolution begins at Lexington, Massachusetts.

MARCH 17, 1776: British troops evacuate Boston, leaving it in American hands for the duration of the Revolution.

JUNE 16, 1780: Massachusetts approves its first state constitution.

FEBRUARY 6, 1788: Massachusetts becomes the sixth state to approve the United States Constitution.

Glossary

ACT: law, so called because it is made by an act of government

ANGLICAN: Church of England, a Protestant church and the state church of England

BANISH: to expel a citizen from his or her country

BOYCOTT: agreement to refuse to buy from or sell to certain businesses

BRITISH: nationality of a person born in Great Britain; people born in England are called "English."

CAMPAIGN: series of actions taken to reach a military goal

CATHOLIC: Roman Catholic; the oldest Christian church organization, governed by a hierarchy based in Rome

CHARTER: document containing the rules for running an organization

DYNASTY: series of rulers from the same family, who pass the throne from one family member to another

EXPORT: to send merchandise out of the country for sale; merchandise sent out of the country

EVANGELIST: traveling preacher who seeks to win converts to a religion by preaching at revival meetings

FRONTIER: newest place of settlement, located the farthest away from the center of population

GREAT BRITAIN: nation formed by England, Wales, Scotland, and Northern Ireland; the term "Great Britain" came into use when England and Scotland formally unified in 1707

HERESY / HERETIC: heresy is a belief that is denounced by one's church / heretic is one who believes in an idea that has been denounced as a heresy

IMPORT: to bring merchandise into the country for sale; merchandise brought into the country

INDIAN: name given to all Native Americans at the time Europeans first came to America, because it was believed that America was actually a close neighbor of India

MILITIA: group of citizens not normally part of the army who join together to defend their land in an emergency

ORTHODOXY: traditional set of beliefs considered by the authorities to be correct

OXEN: plural of ox; neutered bull

PARLIAMENT: the legislature of Great Britain

PATRIOT: American who wanted the colonies to be independent of Great Britain

PLANTER: owner of a plantation, or large farm

PILGRIM: Puritan who separated from the Church of England instead of trying to change it from within

PROTESTANT: any Christian church that has broken from away from Roman Catholic or Eastern Orthodox control

PROVINCIAL: belonging to a province, a territory controlled by a distant authority

PURITAN: Protestant who wanted the Church of England to practice a more "pure" form of Christianity

QUAKER: member of the Society of Friends, a Christian group founded in England around 1650

REFORM: to change for the better

ROYAL GOVERNOR: governor appointed by a king or queen to govern a colony

SACHEM: Algonquian word for chief

SASSAFRAS: type of tree whose bark was used for flavoring or medicinal purposes

SIEGE: campaign to capture a place by surrounding it, cutting it off from supplies, and attacking it

SMUGGLING: secretly and illegally trading in forbidden merchandise, or hiding goods to avoid paying taxes on them

WEST INDIES: islands of the Caribbean Sea, so called because the first European visitors thought they were near India

FURTHER READING

Brenner, Barbara. *If You Were There in 1776.* New York: Bradbury Press, 1994.

Denenberg, Barry. *The Journal of William Thomas Emerson: A Revolutionary War Patriot.* New York: Scholastic, Inc., 1998.

Smith, Carter, ed. *Battles in a New Land: A Source Book on Colonial America.* Brookfield, Conn.: Millbrook Press, 1991.

Smith, Carter, ed. *The Revolutionary War: A Source Book on Colonial America.* Brookfield, Conn.: Millbrook Press, 1991.

Wilbur, C. Keith. *The New England Indians*. Chester, Conn.: Globe Pequot Press, 1990.

WEBSITES

http://www.americaslibrary.gov
Select "Jump back in time" for links to history activities.

http://www.vboston.com/VBoston/Content/FreedomTrail/Index.cfm

http://www.mayflowerhistory.com/

http://www.thinkquest.org/library/JR_index.html
Links to numerous student-designed sites about American colonial history.

BIBLIOGRAPHY

Anderson, Fred. *Crucible of War: The Seven Years' War and the Fate of Empire in British North America, 1754–1766*. New York: Alfred A. Knopf, 2000.

Brown, Richard D. and Jack Tager. *Massachusetts: A Concise History*. Amherst: University of Massachusetts Press, 2000.

Cronon, William. *Changes in the Land: Indians, Colonists, and the Ecology of New England*. New York: Hill & Wang, 1983.

Hawke, David Freeman. *Everyday Life in Early America*. New York: Harper & Row, 1988.

Labaree, Benjamin W. *Colonial Massachusetts: A History*. Millwood, N.Y.: KTO Press, 1979.

Middleton, Richard. *Colonial America: A History, 1607–1760*. Cambridge, Mass.: Blackwell, 1992.

Taylor, Alan. *American Colonies*. New York: Viking, 2001.

The American Heritage History of the Thirteen Colonies. New York: American Heritage Publishing Co., 1967.

INDEX